The Mystery of the Narwhal's Tusk

Early sailors who traveled into the dangerous frozen seas of the Arctic brought home tales of a strange beast with a long spiral horn. They called it the "Arctic unicorn"—but we know it as the narwhal. The narwhal's bizarre tusk is actually not a horn but an extremely sensitive canine tooth, which grows out like a spear.

Scientists have long struggled to understand what purpose the narwhal's tusk serves; this is one of the great mysteries of the natural world. Scientists know that male narwhals sometimes fight with their tusks, and they have also witnessed one narwhal using its tusk to stun a fish. The tusk may also be an ornament, used by the male to impress females. But these are just a few theories, out of many!

FOR MUM AND DAD,
WITH LOVE

JA

FOR HENRY GEGG,
ANNIE RAWSON,
AND GRACE HOGAN,
WITH LOVE

JW

Text © 2022 by Justin Anderson
Illustrations © 2022 by Jo Weaver

First US edition 2022

Library of Congress Catalog Card Number 2021953334
ISBN 978-1-5362-2512-9

22 23 24 25 26 27 APS 10 9 8 7 6 5 4 3 2 1

Printed in Humen, Dongguan, China

This book was typeset in Superclarendon and Tarzana Narrow.
The illustrations were done in charcoal and colored digitally.

Candlewick Press
99 Dover Street
Somerville, Massachusetts 02144

www.candlewick.com

NARWHAL
THE ARCTIC UNICORN

JUSTIN ANDERSON   ILLUSTRATED BY JO WEAVER

CANDLEWICK PRESS

IT is winter in the Arctic. Ice crystals dance in the cold air, shimmering over a frozen sea.

Suddenly a shape explodes out of the water: first one, then another . . .

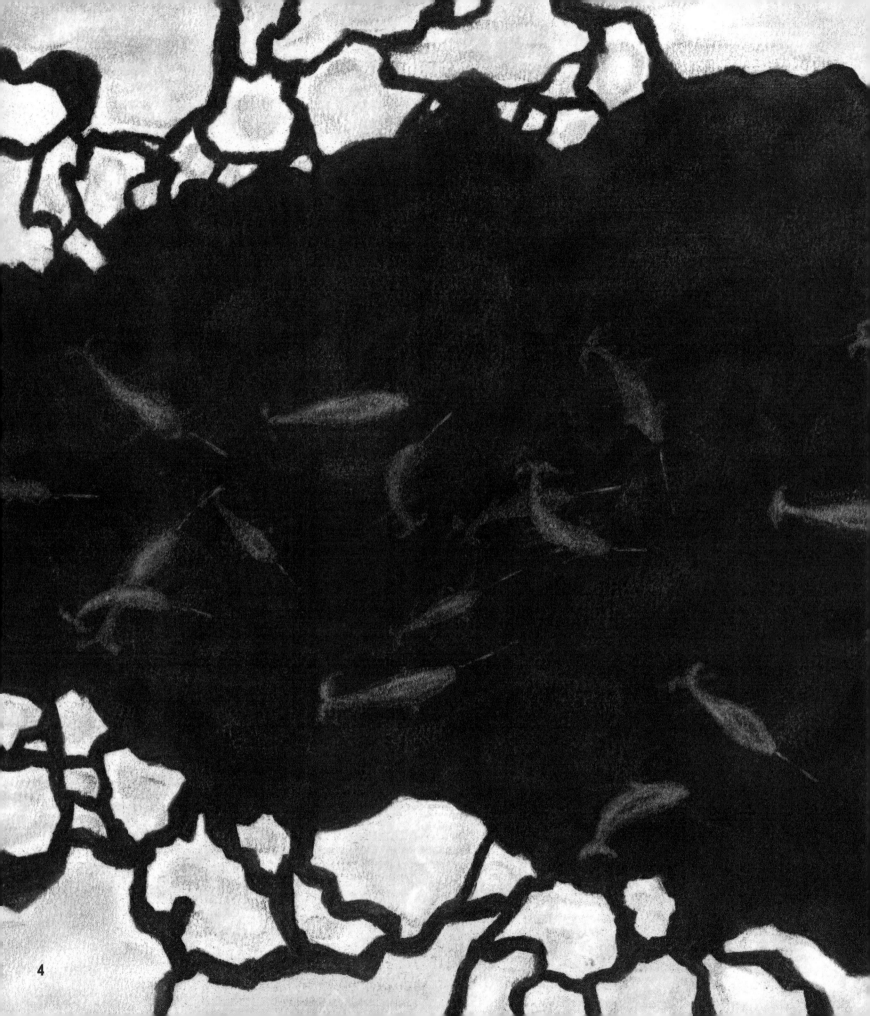

Then more and more shapes appear, until there are
hundreds of them.
   NARWHALS are gathering at the edge of the
ice; their breath clouds the air like fog.
   They have spent the winter here,
   fishing far beneath the frozen ceiling.

Narwhals are toothed whales, related to killer
whales and dolphins. They can reach 16 feet
(5 meters) in length and weigh almost 4,200 pounds
(1,900 kilograms). That's about four times as heavy as a
grand piano!

Primarily males grow the long tusk—only one or two out of every
ten females have a tusk. This might mean narwhals use the tusk
to display to females, like peacocks do with their tails.

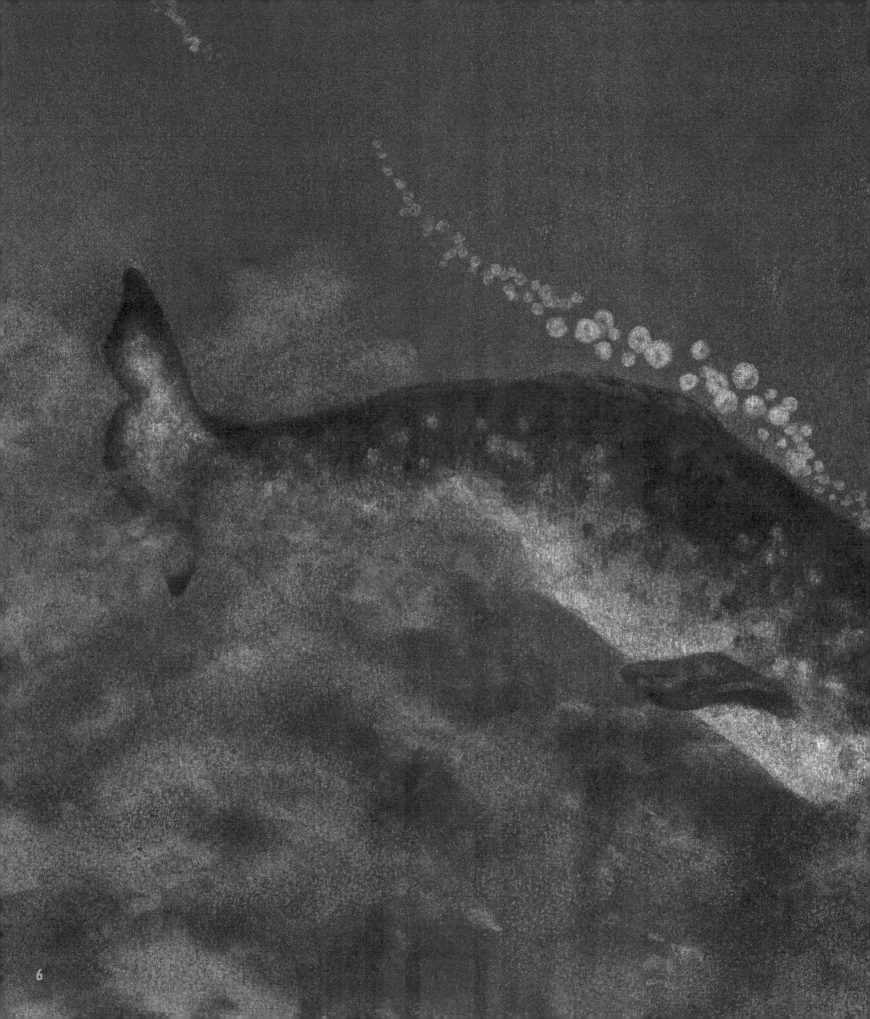

This old narwhal has survived close to fifty winters in these waters. He dives into the darkness. Disturbing a huge flatfish, he gives chase, stirring up clouds of mud from the seabed.

Narwhals can swim close to 5,800 feet (1,800 meters) deep to look for food, diving for twenty-five minutes on a single breath.

The narwhal's remarkable tusk is packed with sensitive nerve endings that some scientists believe might help it to find fish in the darkness. Narwhals don't have any teeth besides their tusk, so they have to use their rubbery lips to suck in fish like a vacuum cleaner.

The wind sweeps in from the south, warming the air.
With a *crack* and a *creak*, the frozen sea begins to melt—
the ice splits apart and a new pathway forms.

Now the narwhals must begin their epic journey north. They will swim for miles, over several months, to the place where they spend their summers. It's a journey with many dangers along the way.

The old narwhal takes a final breath and swims into the maze of ice; his pod follows close behind, their long tusks spearing the waves.

A group of narwhals is called a pod. It has up to twenty members and can be all male, all female, or a mix of both. Sometimes many pods join up, with hundreds of narwhals traveling together.

The wind changes again, and the ice is pushed and pulled by the current. The maze of cracks begins to close and the narwhals' path narrows. They are finally trapped under a single hole in the ice; each narwhal takes its turn to surface, gasping for air.

A polar bear smells their breath on the wind and stalks closer; it's hungry for narwhal meat. The old narwhal must act fast—his pod is in great danger.

Like us, narwhals need air to breathe, which they do through a blowhole on the top of their heads. When the sea is covered by floating ice, it can be hard for narwhals to find a place to take a breath.

With one last breath and a great sweep of his tail,
he dives down beneath the ice to search for a way out.
He makes a series of clicking noises, which bounce
off the ice and then back to him. Narwhals use these
signals like the beam of a flashlight, building pictures
out of sound that help them to "see" in the dark.

Finally he finds an opening, and as he draws closer,
he sees the light pour through. It's an escape route!

Narwhals have small eyes, and their eyesight is poor. Like bats, narwhals use clicking noises to
find their way in the dark. This is called echolocation.

When echolocating, a narwhal can click more than a thousand times per second. Their echolocation skills are thought to be better than any other animal's

The pod continues north for hundreds of miles, following the cliffs and mountains that rise up from the sea like sharp teeth.

Suddenly a loud noise drums across the ice—like two wooden sticks beating together. With his mottled gray head lifted above the water, the old narwhal crosses tusks with another male. It looks like they're having a sword fight!

Jousting is one of the narwhals' strangest behaviors. Some scientists think the males could be fighting to decide who's in charge.

Other scientists think that when narwhals rub their tusks together, it helps to scrape off seaweed . . . perhaps the narwhals aren't jousting but just brushing their teeth!

After many miles, the female narwhals pause on their journey. They have been carrying their babies inside them for more than a year: all through the winter and the long migration north.

Finally it's time to give birth.

Before long, the pod has a brand-new member: a tiny olive-green and brown calf. Without spots or a tusk, he looks like a small sausage!

Narwhal calves stay with their mothers for almost two years and feed on their mothers' milk for the first twenty months.

During their first two or three years, male calves grow a small tusk that is as short as your finger and as thin as a pencil. At eight years old, the tusk can measure more than 6½ feet (2 meters) long. Amazingly, one in every five hundred males will grow two tusks. These "double tuskers" are very rare.

Narwhals eat Greenland halibut, squid, Arctic cod, and shrimp. Scientists have spotted a narwhal using its tusk like a club to hit and stun a fish.

The new calves stick close by their mothers as the pod travels on, until at last they reach the high Arctic islands.

With the summer sun beaming down and the ice almost melted away, the sea is warm and full of new life. The bays are busy with other narwhals and belugas—the white whales of the Arctic.

It's light all day and all night, and the pod can fish around the clock while the newborn calves grow fast on their mothers' milk.

Pure white beluga whales are relatives of the narwhal. They sometimes travel together, and recently a "narluga" (half beluga and half narwhal) was discovered by scientists.

But one morning, a forest of tall dark fins breaks the surface of the water. *Killer* whales. These predators have learned how to hunt the narwhals, listening to their calls to track them.

The old narwhal guides his pod into the shallows, where the bigger killer whales cannot follow. They must stay silent if they are to escape. At last, the killer whales move on; with the danger over for now, the pod is safe once again.

To try to escape these hunters, the narwhals hide in shallow water and stay quiet. Inuit people use the word *ardlingayuk* to describe this behavior; it means "fear of killer whales."

By September, the long summer days have begun to shorten.
Soon the cold of winter will return and the sea will freeze again.
The old narwhal knows it's time to leave before they're trapped
by the new ice. Just a few months old, the young
calves must keep up with the pod.

Back in the deep seas of the south, the narwhals will spend
the winter hunting—until the turning of the seasons.
Then they will make their long journey north once more.

The Future of the Narwhal

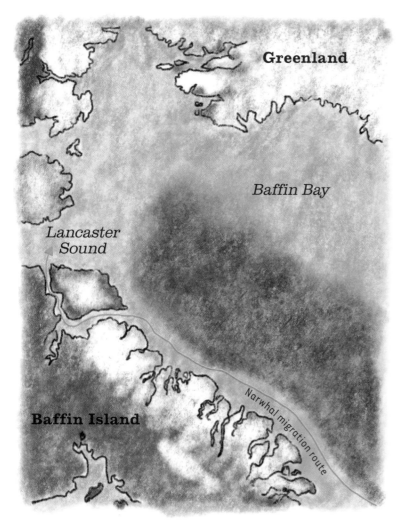

Narwhal Migration Route

By some estimates, there are about eighty thousand narwhals in the wild. That may sound like a lot, but because narwhals live in the remote Arctic, it's hard for scientists to know exactly how many there are and whether their numbers are in danger.

We do know that narwhals are threatened by a changing climate. As the world gets warmer, the sea ice is melting, and changes in the temperature of the seawater might affect where the fish that narwhals like to eat can be found. The narwhals' amazing adaptations allow them to live in the frozen Arctic sea, but with less ice in the summer, the narwhals may begin to encounter more competition for food from other species of whales. And without the sea ice as a barrier, it may also be easier for the narwhals' primary natural predator, the killer whale, to track and hunt them. In the past, the killer whale's huge 6-foot (nearly 2-meter) dorsal fin prevented them from swimming through the ice, but now the path north is easier for them to navigate. Humans are a threat to narwhals, too. The Arctic now sees more boat traffic, and the narwhals could be disturbed by the noise of engines or at risk of colliding with ships. As people further encroach on their habitat, there are also likely to be more oil rigs drilling in the deep water, which could lead to pollution of the narwhals' home.

Further Information

If you want to help make sure that narwhals have a safe future, you can do your best to limit the effects of climate change by saving energy and recycling at home and at school.

For other ways you can help narwhals and to get involved in saving their Arctic home, visit **arcticwwf.org/species/narwhal/**.

For more information from the scientists studying narwhals, visit **staff.washington.edu/klaidre/narwhal-faq/**.

Index

Look up the pages to find out about all these narwhal things.
Don't forget to look at both kinds of word—**this kind** and this kind.